Winston Churchill

and the Second World War.

Sarah Ridley

Lancashire Library Services

30118135242687	
PETERS	J920CHU
£8.99	29-Mar-2018
SCG	

This edition 2013

First published in 2009 by
Franklin Watts
338 Euston Road
London NW1 3BH

Franklin Watts Australia
Level 17/207 Kent Street
Sydney

Copyright © Franklin Watts 2009

Series Editor: Jeremy Smith
Art director: Jonathan Hair
Design: Simon Morse
Cover Design: Jonathan Hair
Picture research: Sarah Ridley

Picture credits: AKG Images: 13.
Bettmann/Corbis: 19. Mary Evans PL: 15.
Fotomas/Topfoto: 9. Fox/Hulton
Archive/Getty Images: 23. Hulton

Archive/Getty Images: front cover 1, 5, 7,
8, 11, 12, 14. Hulton Deutsch/Corbis: 16.
Keystone/Topfoto: front cover r, 1.
Picturepoint/Topham: 18, 21.
Popperfoto/Getty Images: 10, 20.
Sambraus/AKG Images: 4.
Frank Scherschel/Time Life/Getty Images:
22. Topfoto: 6. World History
Archive/Topfoto: 17.

ISBN 978 1 4451 1794 2
Dewey classification: 941.082'092

A CIP catalogue record for this book is
available from the British Library

Franklin Watts is a division of Hachette
Children's Books, an Hachette UK
company.
www.hachette.co.uk

Printed in China

Contents

The Churchill family

Winston Churchill was born on 30th November, 1874. His father was an English lord and his mother was a rich American.

Winston was born at his grandparent's home, Blenheim Palace, near Oxford.

1837

Queen Victoria comes to the throne.

Winston's family home was in London. His father was a Member of Parliament, and both his parents lived very busy lives. Winston did not see much of his parents but he did grow very fond of his nanny.

◀ A photo of Winston's father, Lord Randolph Churchill.

1874 ▶

Lord Randolph Churchill becomes a Member of Parliament (MP).

30 November
1874 ▶

Winston is born.

Early childhood

When Winston was four, the family moved to Ireland. A few years later there was a new baby brother for Winston, called Jack.

◀ Winston as a young boy.

1877 ▶	February 1880 ▶	June 1880 ▶
The Churchill family moves to Ireland.	Jack Churchill is born.	The Churchill family returns to London.

Jack and Winston, on each side of their mother in 1889.

At the age of eight, Winston's parents sent him to boarding school. He hated it and, after two years, he moved to a different school. There he took and passed an exam for a famous school called Harrow.

1882

Winston goes to boarding school.

1887

Queen Victoria's Golden Jubilee.

7

From school to college

The teachers at Harrow School praised Winston's work in English and history. They were not as pleased with his maths, or his timekeeping.

▲ Winston in school uniform. He missed his parents when he was away at school.

1888 ▶

Winston starts at Harrow School.

Winston in his army uniform.

Winston decided he wanted to be a soldier. After leaving school, he went to army college and he did well. Now he took his first army job in India.

1893

Winston starts at an army college (called Sandhurst).

1895

Winston leaves army college. His father and his nanny die.

Adventures abroad

Britain ruled over a huge empire which stretched across the world. The British army helped to protect the Empire. As a soldier in India, Winston was part of this.

Winston was a cavalry officer, a soldier on horseback.

1896 ▶

Winston goes to India.

After India he went to fight in Sudan. Alongside his army life, Winston earned money by writing newspaper reports and history books.

 Winston took part in the Battle of Omdurman in Sudan.

1898

Winston goes to Sudan. The British army win the war there.

1899

The Boer War begins in South Africa.

Into politics

After a few more adventures abroad, Winston decided that he wanted to be a politician. In 1900 he became a Member of Parliament (MP).

In 1908 Winston married Clementine. They had five children.

1900	1901	1905
Winston becomes a Conservative Member of Parliament (MP).	Queen Victoria dies. Edward VII is crowned.	Winston becomes a Liberal MP.

Winston made one big mistake during the war, which resulted in thousands of soldiers dying at Gallipoli in Turkey.

In 1914, the First World War started. During the war, Winston held some important jobs in the government and fought as a soldier for a short time.

1908

Winston and Clementine marry.

1910

Edward VII dies. George V is now king.

1914

First World War breaks out.

The family home

When the First World War ended in 1918, Winston continued as an MP. He shared his time between London and his country home.

Winston enjoyed building walls. Two of his children, Sarah and Mary, are helping here at their home, Chartwell, in Kent.

1918 ▶

The First World War ends.

1922 ▶

Winston and Clementine buy Chartwell, a house in Kent.

During the 1930s Winston began to worry about a man called Adolf Hitler who was gaining power in Germany. Winston feared he would start another world war.

 Adolf Hitler became the leader of Germany in 1933.

1924 ▶

Winston changes back to the Conservative Party.

1933 ▶

Adolf Hitler becomes the German Chancellor.

The Second World War

In 1939, the German
army invaded Poland.
This led to Britain
and France declaring
war on Germany.
The next year,
Winston became the
British Prime
Minister.

Winston gave many
speeches on the radio
and thousands listened.

1936 ▶

George V dies. Edward VIII
is followed by George VI.

1939 ▶

The Second World War
begins.

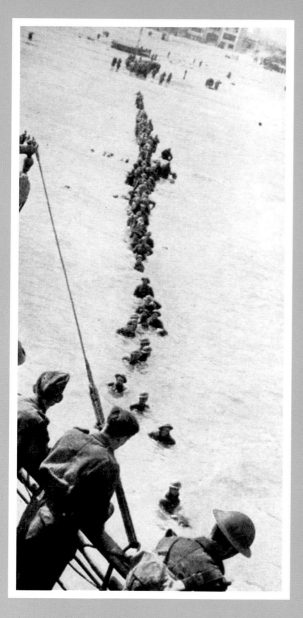

British soldiers wade into the sea from French beaches after the German invasion.

The war was not going well for Britain. Germany had invaded several countries, including France. Winston gave speeches and worked long hours to inspire the British people to keep fighting the Germans.

10 May
1940 ▶
Winston becomes Prime Minister at the age of 65.

1940 ▶
Germany invades many countries.

May 26 - June 4
1940 ▶
British troops are rescued from Dunkirk in France.

Battle of Britain

Some German aeroplanes during the Battle of Britain.

In the summer of 1940, Hitler ordered the German air force to bomb British ports and airfields. For three months the Royal Air Force fought the Germans and beat them.

June
1940 ▶

Italy joins the war on the German side.

Winston visited bombed cities, including Coventry.

However, Hitler could not be stopped that easily. He gave the order to bomb British cities instead. He wanted to make Britain surrender.

 1940

The Battle of Britain. The British and German air forces battle in the air.

1940-1941

Air-raids on British cities.

War around the world

In 1941, Russia and the United States joined the war and battles raged around the world. Winston kept the British people strong, even when the news was bad.

▶ Winston flew around the world to encourage British soldiers and sailors.

1941 ▶
Russia and the USA enter the war.

1942 ▶
Japan wins many battles.

1944 ▶
D-Day Landings. A million US and British troops invade France.

After five long years, the war ended in 1945. Germany had lost. Now the British people wanted a change and Winston lost his position as Prime Minister.

 Winston waves to the crowds on VE Day, the day the war ended in Europe.

June
1945

The Second World War ends.

July
1945

Winston replaced by Clement Attlee as Prime Minister.

June
1947

India gains independence from Britain.

Last years

Winston became Prime Minister once more in 1951. After four years he left this job but he remained a Member of Parliament almost until his death.

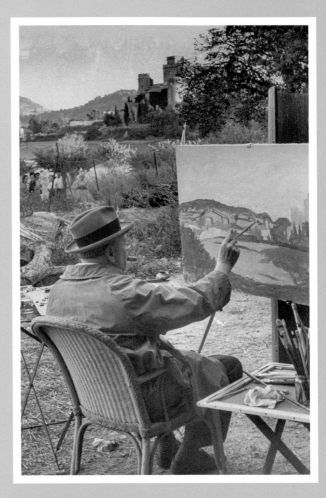

▲ Winston enjoyed painting on holiday, and at home.

1951 ▶	1952 ▶	June 1953 ▶
Winston becomes Prime Minister, aged 76.	George VI dies. Elizabeth II becomes queen.	Coronation of Elizabeth II.

London came to a halt as Winston's coffin was pulled through the streets.

In old age Winston travelled, wrote books, painted and spent time with his large family. He died in 1965 at the age of 90. Remembered as one of the greatest British leaders, his funeral was watched by millions.

December
1953

Winston wins the Nobel Prize for Literature.

1955

Winston resigns as Prime Minister.

24 January
1965

Winston dies, aged 90.

Glossary

Air-raid A bomb attack from aeroplanes.

Boarding school A school where children stay during term time.

Cavalry Soldiers who fight on horseback.

Conservative Party One of the main political parties.

Coronation When a king or queen is crowned.

First World War The world war between 1914 and 1918.

Golden Jubilee The celebration held to mark 50 years of a king or queen's reign.

Hitler Adolf Hitler was the leader of the German National Socialist (Nazi) Party.

Liberal Party One of the main political parties.

Member of Parliament A person elected by voters to represent them in the House of Commons.

Nanny Someone paid to look after the children in a wealthy family.

Prime Minister The leader of the government.

RAF The name given to Britain's Royal Air Force.

Second World War The world war between 1939 and 1945.

Index